The Penguin Chick

Marilyn Woolley

These birds are penguins.
They live by the sea.
It is very cold here.

3

The penguins sit on their nests.
The nests are made from rocks and stones.
The penguins wait for their eggs to hatch.

4

The eggs start to hatch.
Baby penguins are called chicks.
They are gray and fluffy.

This chick is hungry.
One parent goes out to sea
to catch food.
The other parent stays
with the chick.

The parent comes back from the sea.
The parent feeds the chick.
Now the chick is not hungry.

10

When the chick gets bigger,
it will go to sea.
It will take care of itself.

12